PAINTING THE PINK ROSES BLACK

PAINTING
THE PINK ROSES
BLACK

Gerard Smyth

 DEDALUS

THE DEDALUS PRESS
46 Seabury, Sydney Parade Avenue, Sandymount, Dublin 4

ISBN 0 948268 10 7 (paper)

ISBN 0 948268 11 5 (bound)

ACKNOWLEDGEMENTS

Acknowledgements are due to the editors of the following publications where some of these poems, or versions of them, first appeared: In Ireland — The Belfast Review, Cyphers, The Gorey Detail, The Honest Ulsterman, The Irish Times, The Irish University Review, The Irish Press (New Irish Writing), Poetry Ireland Review, Tracks, The Salmon, The Ulster Tatler Literary Miscellany; In Britain — Encounter, Labrys, The Literary Review, The Moorlands Review, Orbis, Other Poetry, Poetry Durham, Poet's Voice; In the U.S. — Adrift, Cream City Review, Illuminations. A number of poems appeared in the booklet *Eclipse* published by Aquila (Isle of Skye) in 1983.

The Dedalus Press acknowledges the assistance of An Chomhairle Ealaíon (The Arts Council) in the publication of this book.

Typesetting & make-up: Vermilion
Cover design: Brendan Foreman

Contents

1

On the Way................................... 9
Corca Bascinn................................. 10
Voices....................................... 11
Realm....................................... 12
The West.................................... 13
Village...................................... 14
Hen Woman.................................. 15
Fisherwife................................... 16
Ghost Forge................................. 17
Lapse....................................... 18
Reminiscence................................ 19
Deathwatch.................................. 20
Requiem..................................... 21
Samhain..................................... 22
Quest....................................... 23
Sanctuary................................... 24

2

On the Outskirts.............................. 27
Our House................................... 28
Sketch...................................... 29
Loneliness................................... 30
Gale.. 31
Lovers...................................... 32
Eclipse...................................... 33
Insomnia.................................... 34
Face to Face................................. 35
During an Illness............................. 36
Fever....................................... 37
Storytime.................................... 38
Prelude..................................... 39
Phoenix Park................................ 40
Liffeyside 1957.............................. 41

Viking Ground............................... 42

Home Truths............................... 43

3

'Little Flower'............................... 47

Pentecost............................... 48

About the Wounds........................ 49

Temple............................... 50

Byzantium............................... 52

Interlude............................... 53

To the memory of Frances Smyth (1902-1982)

1

ON THE WAY

We are on a train going toward the sea.
The names of the stations are halfway
between two languages. The landscape is grim,
as if waiting for an attack.
Everything's in place.
Everything lies there without moving:
the mud at the bottom of the lake, the sand
that has stepped ashore.
The stillness asks us what we are doing
with our souls.

A shadow like a long funeral
accompanies the train.
Villages, cemeteries go in tandem after each other.

The carriage is crowded:
there are many hands worn out from waving goodbye.
The dream-faces in the carriage window
have eyes that left their gaze somewhere else
far behind.
       The window is open, letting in
       a freedom the width of the whole horizon.

CORCA BASCINN
for J.L.

None can leave and none may enter
the stone circle pitched like the ruins of empire.
And who is left to listen to rainfall
on the fresh tar at evening
on a road disappearing over the edge of cliffs.

Nothing equals the desolation
of the house where mist does not stop at the threshold.
The holy wells run dry —
drop by drop the thirst of those who've drunk
from them is multiplied.

The bleached rocks hide
flowers cowering from the sickle
and the hermit whose fear is the existence of others.
The stump of the cross, the castle that crumbles
shall rise again
            in the child's book of colours.

VOICES

Not everything silent is dumb:
not the ancient rock drawing, not the river
of fishes tethered to icy darkness.

There is misery in the winter ditch
and in the hedges linking field to field.
It is not natural: the mist
dissolving distance, the pallor of the sun.
There is weariness
and light that's dimmer than the underworld.

The megalith that does not move is petrified
and purple. On the river
the rustle of a swan sounds crisp
and broken-spirited.

Smoke from the chimneys and the foam of the sea
are kept in motion by the same laws.
Stone takes flight from the quarry
with an echo that's perilous
like thunder on a day of wrath.

REALM
(i.m. Francis Ledwidge)

Land of unbolted doors
and the coolness of rainwater.
On the royal roads carts trundled
carrying the mysteries of the dungheap.

The chill of the riverbank
was chased away
by blasts from the hunter's horn.
In the nettle wilderness
a cottage stump gave back its mud walls
to the earth. There you heard
the song of the chicken roost,
found fox-tracks
down the narrow furrows of clay.

The mower's blade clawing at ditches
drew blood from fruit of the bramblebush.
By night the apple sky
in the orchard fell down,
buttermilk in the pantry changed semblance.

THE WEST

The wind alone is walking the roads of the west,
it lashes the emerald hillside parishes.
Out where stone settlements are withering
I sense vigilance —

the vigilance of enemies watching each other,
eavesdropping on the opposite side of the frontier.

In spring the upturned earth is a wound
on the landscape. Cloud-shadow crosses the sea.
The atmosphere creaks like the coffin-ships
once lured to a future too far away.

VILLAGE

In the village foodstore everything looks good
— it is like the table laid for a homecoming.

Most of the villagers live and die unnoticed,
they pass time waiting for the feast days.

The infrequent stranger who strays among them
always asks the way to the next village.

There is nothing taller than the wondrous church,
it is motionless and imperturbable.

Deeds of christening, marriage and death rot away
in the register. Dreams cross the threshold

to fill the cottages with the imaginary, the dread
and wonder of what-might-have-been.

HEN WOMAN

You cross yourself when you're told
that forklightning scorched a man
in the next parish, left a wall scarred
and made a silhouette of straw and stone.

After the downpour
soft ground is cooking in the sun,
rainwater floats on cold enamel.
After a night of augury
your apron pockets fatten with eggs
collected from haystack and dunghill.

Balancing unspilled water in two buckets
full to the brim
is a trick learned in youth:
you perform it well,
your knuckles turning to the colour of iodine.

In shadows of furniture you are left
remembering that the meek
shall inherit the earth. It's a simple world
of right and wrong. Gold wears off the rim of the cup
you drink from.

FISHERWIFE

Draped in the black warmth
of a shawl, she feels
the coolness of crockery
and the crackling heat
of the pan. The light
falling down the chimney
is a tongue that dampens
soot and smoke.

In the seashore house
there are ships in bottles.
The walls give off an odour
of caps and coats hung to dry.

In summer weeks go by
without the lamps
being filled with oil:
the days are gradual
like the time required
to forget a tragedy
— death by water,
a disappearance on the horizon.

GHOST FORGE

A nest of nails where hammers descended
striking iron,
releasing an iron fragrance.
Where stains of fire proliferated
the anvil's withered down to its roots.

The pitcher under the water-tap
has a chipped mouth.
Ash scooped out of the brazier
shall never cool
nor shall the glow on the forehead
of the horseshoe-maker.

Sparks that fluttered, dazzling his eyes,
have become still now,
stored up as embers in the folds of an apron.
The bellows' breath is gone,
dried up in the pungence of smoke.

LAPSE

Dust from their shoes has left the mark of steps
outdistanced by destiny.
Metamorphosis devours the windowframes
and threshold
   of grandmother's house.

Upon the wall flames interchange
in a burning bush that speaks of nothing.
A light breeze shakes the latch
(perhaps it's the sound of the second coming?)

Stripped of their true marriage
stone from stone breaks loose.
Through the rotted nuptial chamber
saints' names,
   disguised as children, vanish.

Neither glow nor glimmer keep vigil
where wax from candles has grown hard and brittle.

Doors off their hinges reveal no flesh
but a visible spirit.
   In the mirror absence chills
whoever seeks an image.

REMINISCENCE

I *Evensong*

From the door I saw unending distance,
crossroads where nothing happened.
It seemed like the age before cars.

The comforting noise of milk filling a bucket
came from the shadow-world.
It was milking-time in the country,
the hour I loved. Darkness crowded the henhouse,
I was afraid to enter. The bolt was drawn
to guard against the prowling vixen.

II *Childhood House*

In the kitchen everything shone:
linoleum, china, the stacked dresser.
Smoke discoloured the wall it clung to
and the hearthstone under the dreaming dog.

Grandmother — her ages of grief thickening —
had a deep distrust of electricity.
With great patience she combed the hair
falling to her shoulders.

Late at night
dance-music rose up from the wooden radio.
The calmed-down fire forsaken until cock-crow
was enough to keep the chill outside
in the crevices
and treetops brimming with heaven's breeze.

DEATHWATCH

The vigil clock,
the one with the power to increase exhaustion,
was ticking away, gathering momentum.
Cigarette burns on the bedside table
were like eyesockets with no eyes in them.

I remember refusing to look
at the instruments of the sickroom:
crucifix, candles, holy water.
The glow of the lamp was lowered to a smaller
sombre light detached from most of the room.

Daybreak trickled into the darkness.
I heard the hooves
of all the repeated, unriddable questions
stampeding towards you
out of the stillness and down from the rafters.

Red ash shifted in the ramshackle fire.
The flutter of mothwings against the window
slowly expired.

REQUIEM

Between the headstones a passageway
deliberately leads us back . . . here, the worm
goes deeper, away from the daylight lamp.

Do not compare to dream
the accidental gathering of figures
in the landscape.
   The flowers.
The bell faintly shimmering —
brief dance of its unwithering bronze.

Wind on the balcony intones a tangible requiem.

Stone
(stiff with the calm composure of eternity)
has guessed your name,
your age: the essential details
of the transience of a lifetime.

In the nest of ashes and earth
your face grows pale till there's nobody there.
Noboay and nothing.

Thinking back, looking with half-closed eyes
I dimly see you —
cooking, cleaning, buttering bread,
coping with the scarcity of divine help.

SAMHAIN

Giggling children beg for apples
and threaten us with druid magic.
Dew on the window is a dense mask
covering the face of Venus.
The fire consumes dry twigs.
On the far side of kitchen glass
the barren winter trees
are like chimeras at the road's verge.

The storyteller
is steeped in the lore of *samhain*.
Bat and barn owl scatter
tipping the bushes and tunnelling the dark.
The granaries are under hoarfrost.

In whitewashed chapels
organ-notes divulge a mood of lamentation.
In the morning there'll be time enough
to sweep away the charred remains
of bonfires fed with winterwood.

QUEST
for Ewart Milne

On the traveller's shoulder a tear
belonging to the stay-at-home dreamer.
On his lap the perspective
of a different land:
maplines showing which direction leads
out of the labyrinth.

The light of the house built on water
shines and blinds. On the night-ferry
some sleep, others read:
their hearts taste the hunger of characters
out of Dickens and Dostoevsky.

It is always the same leaving the harbour,
there's a *deja vu* presence
of something felt before —
in the cinema, say, watching a film
about the quest for a better life.

SANCTUARY

Tired at nightfall we curse the key
that doesn't fit the lock.
There at the horizon
earth and sky kiss profusely.
Clusters of parched leaves
hang over ditches
— soon they'll spill into our laps.

A wail shakes the children's room
— we identify it
as the effort it takes to flee
from a nightmare. In the copper light
of half-past-nine
the noise of the living drains away.

The road seems thinner.
Cooking smells brush the window,
they pass through its transparency.
The splendour-colours
of dishes and cutlery form a circle,
a table of intimacy to which we return
tired at nightfall.

2

ON THE OUTSKIRTS

We give names to the noises of the road
— *car, bus, ambulance.*
Like the people in the crucible of society
the foundation stones
have no breathing space between them.
Through the high-tension cables
goes the menacing hum
of electricity in search of a home.

A flame sprouts from embers and sticks
and one of us looks out
at drying clothes painted on mid-air.
The child with crusted sores
falls for the hundredth time today.
The postman is pushing lies
through a letterbox.

We give names to the noises of the street
— *dogbark, banging door.*
The cistern's snatch of song is vehement.
The thud of hobnailed boots gets heavier
— it's the rubbish-collector
coming to share our secrets.

OUR HOUSE

The radio-singers at night
were our nearest neighbours. In the quiet
we could hear the reverberations
of a feather falling.

On mornings when it was still dark
the effulgence of the bulb was stark
and painful. Cups and saucers
slammed on the table
woke me and drove me out of myself.

We came here in nest-building time.
Wind in the chimney was more volatile
than the word that came down
in tongues of fire.

The cooker flared into four rings of flame.
Every noise was purposeful:
the stutter of the sewing-machine,
the spin-dryer tossing
loose change left in a pocket.

SKETCH

The hole in the wallpaper is a wound that festers.
Water in the kettle is almost on fire.
There are dark circles round the eyes of the rooks,
they taste the soporific garden smoke and sleep.

We wake to music penetrating the ether,
to fresh milk, food and warmth.
In the morning, the first steps we take
are to the bathroom: there, the light is candid
from floor to ceiling,
the roof is fragile where dampness seeps through.

At night the Virgin in the gilded frame
listens to coughing that darkens the room.
The smell of time is on the linen
wrapped around us.
We doze. There is no connection
between the dream and what happens in life.

LONELINESS

Rain sings a requiem in the knacker's yard.
At the edge of wasteland
a child's plaything is discarded, suddenly
and forever. Instead of smoke
chimneys shed the soul-stifling melancholy
of nights at the end of June.

the clock strikes; its twelve chimes hypnotise.
Over an unfinished game of chess
someone says Goodnight. The light
of the apple-blossom is snatched away.
Watchdogs blend with the quiet behind closed
        windows.

Everyone's at rest
except the girl sewing moonbeams to a garment.
The house of glass glowing in the dark
is the last bus with only a few travellers
going back to where they began.

GALE

Firelight attracts a draught from the window.
The flame on the wick gasps for breath —
like the ghost-flesh of apparitions
it flickers and fades. The gale is everywhere —
it can pass through the eye of a needle
or move heaven nearer to earth.
Once more the pillow under your head absorbs
the weeping that is part of marriage.

After midnight the quieter sounds strive
to be heard: the grains of dust,
the soapy water dripping from dresses and shirts.
Sugar on the table gleams like frost.
The quick smile of a neighbour withdraws
behind a curtain. We lie still, expecting a pause
in the movement that carries life forward.

LOVERS ✓

We lie down and the walls rise up.
The lurking mouse discovers nothing edible
in the cupboards. On your bare back
the moon has dropped the pallor of its face.

Nails and hammer, shovel and pick
have been put aside. The hush is diaphanous
and broken only by the bark
of a dog which can't keep its voice in its mouth.

We are never prepared for that sudden visit
of sound to our ears. Behind closed eyelids
there's nothing to be heard. How empty the world is
and in it the gigantic throbbing of our hearts,

the stillness is the gesture of things in common —
like the stillness in the belly of the Trojan Horse.

ECLIPSE

I

In the lull between Monday and Tuesday
when the heart's more heavy than a dead tree
you strip completely —
down to the look of love that makes no sound
but signals to me like a distant fire.

With the candour of a dictionary the moon describes
inertia's face.
It is about that time when moths catch flame
when milk turns sour after ageing.

II

The child in bed with only darkness to read
lies still in mute self-wonder
— listening to leaves of the forest
in dialogue with the beyond.
He is heir to more than promises can give.

Eyelids and fingertips
diminutive but strong:
a stem that will not break in the midst of storm.

On pillows bright as mother's milk
wide coolness spreads to hair untouched by autumn

and the child in the chamber of August heat
awakes with no wish to remember his dream
but to drink from water
moon-coloured like the blaze on his forehead.

INSOMNIA

The glass reddened by wine is best seen
in the dark. Your shadow disconnected from mine
leaves a blank space
consumed by the light —
the phosphorescent light of the table lamp.
The ring on your finger, the thought in your eye
have a lustre that's identical.
I glance upwards: the cross with its unmourned Christ
reminds me that the word Love
is about preparing to die. . . . The dead
in the sepia photograph of my parents' wedding
look happy. The house fills up
with their perfect calm.
To pass time I imagine the ghost-life
to which they've vanished.

FACE TO FACE

A moment ago in winter monotony
I thought I saw the sun's last ray.
Child's-play is over
and round the house old timbers creak,
conjuring a revenant.

Face to face we rectify
misdeeds of passion . . . the curse that flew
from rancorous mouths is now erased
and now our senses keep a rendezvous
of touch and taste.

Nightlong the moon falls from its place.
The room is laden
with fragrance and hallucination.
Rain on the window reaches the heart:
downpour and diminuendo

make a wavering chant of invocation
to our domain.
Beneath an intimate gathering of flame
we grow interlaced —
bodies consumed by their twin cadence.

DURING AN ILLNESS

Curtain cloth
blindfolds the house.
Hands of the clock
move forward
with feebler and feebler effort.
The chimes are wearying
at noon and midnight.

The pillow,
white for tranquillity,
has been warmed
by the sun that shines
too little or too much.

In the room
of the daytime sleeper
the struggle against sleep
waxes and wanes.
Flowers grieve
for their lost fragrance.
Bluebottles round
uneaten fruit
are giddy with impatience.

FEVER

The windows of the hospital reflect a lunar calm.
Nightsmoke from the boiler-house
swirls in muted agitation. In a corner
of the fever-ward geraniums that were wilting
bloom — it is the only miracle,
the only sign of a life not thwarted by lassitude.

Soup thick as ointment broods in a bowl,
stiffened bread lies mouldering. The silence now
is a nightingale empty of sound.
The sick child wakes after falling
through the deepness of space:
he feels the leadweight of eyelids
half-opening to the present. At midnight,
when the youngest face wears the oldest expression,
the dark is perfect:
                    it paints the pink roses black.

STORYTIME

A little hand elevates the book —
the apocrypha we accept without proof.
I taste it
and feel on my tongue the magnetic pull
of stories that pass from generation

to generation.
Magic and wickedness get into your eyes,
the wolf from the fable is eating your flesh.
Forgetting yourself
you step into the white space of imagination

between the words.
Your nocturnal dress has you ready for sleep.
Listening, you are like the birds
at their garden feast
gathered round the crumbs and the worms.

PRELUDE

Perceptible at dawn, our breaths
rising and falling. Our touchable existence
barely audible above the din
of nomads seeking new frontiers —
their going pierces those of us who stay.

Each day the ritual of welcoming the invisible.
Music that was missing takes form again:
a tide of echoes imposed by morning traffic.

A step away from translucence,
the last star smoulders in the market place.
Somewhere a siren obliterates
lethargy and lullaby. We are in the kitchen
and in my waking-dream the snowdrift
is a woman's body, naked and bone-chilling.

Our discourse throbs like the sea in winter.
This morning, God in the flesh
must be this coolness sketched from lawn to lawn,
faint sounds of frost unlocking.

PHOENIX PARK
for Simon

Like an astronomer looking for new stars
you peer fixedly
into the zenith of green branches.
A chill sits on the park benches.
Not even a handful of chestnuts are left
after the early marauding thief.

The deer watching from soaked grass
are statues imitating stillness and grief.
The stag's breath seems inexhaustible
after his gallop in front of the wind.

Evil and miry
the sky's nest is fathom-deep in the pond.
A feather drifts from the corpse of a swan.
Bread on the water floats in clusters.

LIFFEYSIDE 1957

The imprint that bodies make is still on the mattress
dumped out for incineration.
The gulls possessed by the voices of Babel
keep calling and calling . . .

Dozens of lights switched on
create the illusion of a spirited blaze.
The man in blue overalls seems to be watching
for a change in the behaviour of old machinery.
Butcher and baker hold back their secret:
is it that food is not enough
to nourish a family?

In warehouse and workshop
the deaf-and-dumb shadows of metal and wood
stand shoulder to shoulder.
The odour of yeast is indestructible
in yards at the back of the brewery.

VIKING GROUND

Cathedral on the Viking ground. The crypt
contains the arid quiet of a hiding-place.

Pigsqueels in the slaughterhouse.
Brickdust trickling down.
Black railings gird the gaping emptiness
of the park in February.

The foodbringer fetches bread
still cooling
still luminous with heat from the ovens.
The timber merchant's men
are busy judging and splitting tree-trunks.

Chimneys. Church bells.
Pigeons test the sharpness of a roof's apex.

The rows of houses have their secret thoughts.
Breath from inside the rooms
keeps appearing on windows swollen with frost.

HOME TRUTHS

The child-corpse,
small as a loaf of bread, vanished
leaving a stillness in the family.
The atmosphere smelled of bronchitis medicine,
it was the atmosphere of the nineteen-fifties.

In the spirit world of the Church of Saint Nicholas
I wanted to trust
the stoic and long-bearded saints
painted on the ceiling.

One evening I felt a change:
the homely look was missing from table and chairs,
wet clothes stiffened
over a gas flame (the sign
of a man doing his wife's work.)

The slow walk of father's widowhood
entered the street —
everything about him was boarded up.

3

'LITTLE FLOWER'
for Padraig J Daly

It was a mutable world.
Flowers rotted and water grew stale.
Each day began with ceremony,
kneeling women sang praise

and heard, far-off,
the barely audible footsteps on the road
to Emmaus.
        Thérèse
what shudders of doubt clung to you
as dust was shaken from the empty shroud?

In your soul-diary
anguish, affliction, quiet distress:
the page was full
in which the troubles of Job
changed to smaller dimensions.

PENTECOST

Hear the breeze of visitation hovering
above the house.

Everywhere, the phenomena
of wonder: treeless leaves, stripped branches —
the unbeliever only half-aware
of birdsong becoming intransient . . .

Put out the light and there's another light
that startles.

Self-radiant child,
in your child's-head a pastoral tenderness;
in your unfeigned smile
there's someone back from the dead

— who's seen the truth
            and solved the mysteries.

ABOUT THE WOUNDS
i.m. Janos Pilinsky

About the wounds of passion week,
about the cross but not the cross
worn as a piece of jewellery
you were wondering —

can this suffice
for man's delight in his five senses?

Inviolable like the sun
and never consumed
the unhealed stigma blooms and blooms,

shedding itself until you stop believing.

TEMPLE

I

Whose eyes are these that gaze and gaze
from sculpted solitude
— fading from icon and pieta?

It is getting dark.
Dusk has half-erased the house of God.
From nowhere comes the voice
of supplication, pleading
at the edge of light and refuge.

Out of the depths and from echoing hill
earth's cries
invoke the unsealed sepulchre
    where death consoles the living.

II

Silencing all questions
the smoke of incense hoists a chant
of joyous Easter Latin.

Brass and bronze have the appearance of gold.
The bones of statues
are radiant in light from another world.

The entry door looms up —
when it opens the air divides,
wisps of air breathe down the nave
of brooding quietness.

Stone rises to reach the sky.
Where sunlight collides with chapel glass
a hermit stands in fire
reciting, perhaps, the last of the psalms.

BYZANTIUM

Sometimes whole families
come, hoping to find Golgotha
or wooed by the ceremonial silk and gold —
the glittering treasure stored up
to be destroyed.

Invisible still
the difference between the consecrated
and unconsecrated wine.
The ravaged candles make a smoky sign:
hotter the wax while the flame is ebbing
to final darkness.

Closed doors cannot keep the devil out.
In my mouth is the taste of lamb's blood
and salt in which to preserve
the prophet's word.

INTERLUDE

Looking at thorn I think
of the thorn-covered God. I sit and listen.
An insect-wing is scratching the wall.
My wristwatch, ticking obstinately,
sends out a sound like a clenched
fist hammering and hammering.

In the yard a bony chicken
is picking at patches of sunlight.
Implements of the fields are going rusty
where the moist weather touched them.

Today we are submerged in the requiem
music of Good Friday.
The tree with its back turned to the house
is tranquil, as if it were dead.
Tomorrow
we'll be at each other's throats again.